Gifts of Love, Treasures of Life

By
David Slater

Gifts of Love, Treasures of Life

Author: David Slater

Copyright © 2025 David Slater

The right of David Slater to be identified as author of this work has been asserted by the author in accordance with section 77 and 78 of the Copyright, Designs and Patents Act 1988.

ISBN 978-1-83538-605-7 (Paperback)
    978-1-83538-606-4 (E-Book)

Cover Design and Book Layout by:
    White Magic Studios
    www.whitemagicstudios.co.uk

Published by:
    Maple Publishers
    Fairbourne Drive, Atterbury,
    Milton Keynes,
    MK10 9RG, UK
    www.maplepublishers.com

A CIP catalogue record for this title is available from the British Library.

All rights reserved. No part of this book may be reproduced or translated by any form or by any means, electronic or mechanical, including photocopying, recording or by any information storage and retrieval system without written permission from the author.

The views expressed in this work are solely those of the author and do not necessarily reflect the views of the publisher, and the publisher hereby disclaims any responsibility for them.

Dedication

*This book is for my late, beloved and
missed so immensely, Gaynor.*

*She was a light, a warming presence that when
I hurt or injured myself (I have neuropathy,
muscle wasting and heart disease) after a fall
or clumsy fingers and cutlery, she tended my wounds.*

*Now alone, I move slower, counting steps well ahead of
moving otherwise, oops! over I go.*

*Her humour, intelligence, caring, her love of nature which
endowed her with the pet name... Dormouse.
She cared about people.*

*And we loved each other very deeply.
That is why the title of the book.*

*So my darling Gaynor, this is for our
Love's Gifts and Life's Treasures we shared.*

I am yours for eternity my love.

Your Whalish Whale.

Contents

Gaynor 9

All Around 10

Cry, Cry, Cry 11

Dream Girl 12

When 13

Days 14

Floating 15

Heartbreak Tree 16

Misted Eyes 17

Moon Promises 18

Everyone Must Have A Dream 19

Dream World 20

Wonder 22

Fairness 23

Love Story 24

'If' Says A Lot 25

Spellbound 26

It Is Tender 28

Little Dormouse 29

There Is A Song 30

No Box of Chocolates 31

Dreams	33
Dreams #2	34
A Little Poem	35
Dance Time	36
Tender Is The Touch	38
Final Breath	39
Buttercup	40
Will You	41
Days of Promise	43
Flowers and Butterflies	45
Walk With Me	46
The Frontier	48
Your Gift	50
I Would Kneel	52
If I Had Arms As Long As Time	53
The Unicorn	54
Patterns	56
Featherlight	57
Words of Love	58
The Master Magician	59
The Waters	61
The Cave of Broken Hearts	63
The Shipwrecks	65

Insidious Creature	67
Love Sweet, Love sour	69
Cost of Some Childhoods	71
Washing Waters	72
Forever	73
How Dry The Seas Are	75
To Be Here With Dormouse	76
The Seasons	77
Oh! Muse	78
Empty Spaces?	80
Love Conquers	81
Winds	82
When The Garden Blooms For Dormouse	84
Menu of Meaning	85
Tis' There	86
Just Like Galadriel	88
House of Shared Emotion	89
Timestreams	91
We Are All Children	92
Time Runs Forever	93
More Than Love	94
Stardust and Moonglow	96
I Flicker	97

In The Velveteen Stream	98
The Reel of Film	99
Memories	101
Déjà vu	103
This House (A short story in prose)	105
Words Of Songs Hit A Chord	107
Photographs of You	108
Where You Reside	110
Legends	111
How Big Sadness Is	112
Dreams and Actual Reality	113
Underhanded Cards	115
It Is Tender (2)	117
The Light	118
Betwixt	119
How It Is...Is Not As It Was	120
Mirrors	122
When A Heart Breaks	124
Mellow Is The Music.	125
Winds	127
In Candlelight	128
Begone	130
Oh My Dearest	132

It Is A Sad House 134

Echoes 135

Lonely For You 137

The Record Player 139

Inspirational Woman 141

What Makes A Man Great 143

The World Could End 145

Companionship 146

The Rocking Horse 147

Landscapes of Life 149

Sing A Song 150

Gaynor's Moon 151

Gaynor

Gaynor, that special light
The sweetest song ever sung
Heard within birdsong
And wherever bells are rung
The most perfect notes
In timbre and pitch
Swirling amongst woodlands
Hills, meadows, hedge and ditch
Floating upon oceans
Skimming seas
Truer than all sworn oaths
Sweeter than honey from bees
The Lady of Golden Heart
My beloved that I miss so much
Finer than porcelain
Softer than silk to the touch.

10/11/24

All Around

Grief is all around
In the open
Under rocks in the ground
Hidden away
It's by age, or illness
Or someone's wicked hand
Grief is all around us
That we understand
Though it drains the heart and soul
We still try to carry on regardless
But the evenings bring such awful silence
Incompatible, incompanionable and lacking warmth and finesse.
Grief is all around
Carried in the air
You can see it on wan faces
In the lackluster stare
Upon a person's demeanor
Though they try to conceal
Also in their carriage
You can see, if you truly look, the way they feel
And though it sits upon them like a shawl
They try to make of it, the best
But grief is their companion daily
Until their final rest.

9/2/25

Cry, Cry, Cry

Cry, cry, cry
Wear the grief as a badge of love
Cry, cry, cry
Until the seas run dry
Cry those tears, cry
Until your eyes are empty
Cry, cry, cry
Until they are like the deepest desert is dry
Just cry
No matter what triggers those tears
Just cry
And let your most beautiful love show
Cry, cry, cry
Let your light blind and grow
Cry, cry, cry
For your loved ones are worth every teardrop
That you let fall from your eyes.

5/2/25-updated 13/2/25

Dream Girl

If it wasn't for your photographs
All your clothes, books and music upstairs
Other bits and pieces
I'd think that you and me were a dream
That I'd had and have every night
So many times I look about me
Your absence just makes it all a dreamscape Unreal.
The fact of your not being here a gigantic exclamation mark
And the fact is we were
We were together
You were and still are my life's love
My Dream girl.
It feels as if it was a dream because of how much I miss you
How much I long to hug and hold you.
It won't be a dream I know
When we meet again
But until then
It's a nightmare.

7/1/25

When

When I'm really down
Do you see it and try to hold me?
When I'm crying, which is often
Do you try to comfort me, soothe me?
When I'm bruised by knocks
Do you wish you could speak to me?
And when I'm cut after a stupid accident with a knife or floor
Do you want to dress the wound?.
When I'm struggling to eat properly
Do you wish you could cook me something I can digest?.
Whe I'm just laying back and staring at the TV or your photographs
Do you wish you could make me laugh properly again?.
When I'm tired of living this way
Do you want to tell me to battle on?
When I want to go to bed not long after getting up
Do you wish you could tuck me up in bed and sing me to sleep?.

Knowing you my love, my darling Gaynor, you do
And I wish you could
But then if you could do those things then you'd be here
And I wouldn't be going through all that and needing the answer.

Miss you my love, never is such a small world so huge
It does not encompass how I feel.

29/12/24

Days

Days slip by and we shake our heads
Focusing on the new day and what it may bring
Me,
I shake my head and look back
Holding tight and for my life
To the you that is there
The you who was absent for so long from this house
The you, your family, I and this house and contents miss.
I hold tight to the days that are our history
Have since you slipped away on your golden journey to peace
Your journey out of pain and discomfort
My memory seeking out to pinpoint moments
To zoom in on those special, warm times of us.
I hold them tight
Hearing again your voice in my mind
My heart wreaking havoc on my emotions
Oh those days may be past
But they are my now too
Also they will be my future
Burrowing down into those treasured moments
Days irreplaceable
Immeasurable
All.

21/12/24

Floating

Floating
Within memories
Within dreams
Endlessly enveloped in your arms
Endlessly skimming streams.
Floating
Within love
Within emotions
Endlessly feeling your heartbeat
Endlessly we swim in oceans.
Floating
Forever without losing the sensation
Without losing the light that you shine
Without forgetting one iota of your being
Without losing those memories that I call mine.
Floating
With you my beloved
Eternally our beautiful life together
Floating with you darling Gaynor
Through time forever.

8/12/24

Heartbreak Tree

I scatter seeds as I go
Wandering far and wide, broad and long
Planting those children of the soil
And sing my heartbreak song.
Now years have passed
And though I wander the earth no more
Those seeds almost all failed to grow
But one did truly spore.
Where it grew with branches
Broad and long, firm and strong
And as you near this solitary oak
You'll hear it sing my heartbreak song.
The moor that it graces looks bleak
Though suits the trees spirit so wild and free
For it sings of the lady I beloved
Sings its heartfelt most for me.
The heartbreak tree will last anon
Let it seeds blow wild and free
And in time the songs will entwine
Songs of love, songs of you and me.

30/11/24

Misted Eyes

Misted eyes
Echoes of unheard good-byes
Though I know we speak even now
My words reaching you
Your love enfolding me from out of the blue.
Misted, damp eyes
Silent unlimited nighttime cries
Following on from daytime weeps
Me always apologising for those unleashed emotions
Rippling over the spacial/ethereal oceans.
Misted eyes
Unspoken goodbyes
Feelings of my failing
Not there to kiss and bid adieu…for now
But I know you feel my love… somehow.

10/11/24

Moon Promises

There are ' Harvest Moons '
'Hunters Moons '
Even ' Witches Moons '
But where oh where is the ' Lover's Moon '
All moons are for lovers
Whether quarter, half, three quarter or full
Blue, white or blood
They all bear witness to love
But be truthful under the moon when making promises
When plighting your troth
For the moon is the watcher for the Goddess of Love
And expects honesty
Faithfulness
Words spoken of love thus
Are ironbound
So if you are the flighty sort then words spoken under the luminous orb
Are best not uttered
Ill words are best buttered on bread and swallowed
So be advised.
I told my love often she was the love of my life
And those words are rimmed in fire and gold
And even since she went to sleep
I make that statement daily
She is
And always will be…THE ONE.

28/10/24

Everyone Must Have A Dream

Everyone has a dream
Everyone needs a dream
To help them through their days.
I have a dream
But I know it won't become reality
For some dreams are impossible to make true.
My dream
That Gaynor will come through the front door
And all the clothes in bags upon her bed
That came back from the hospice
She will put back in their rightful place.

That is my dream.
Everyday I wish it to happen.
I know it is impossible
But it is my dream
And everyone must have a dream
No matter how impossible it is.
It keeps me alive.

23/10/24

Dream World

The one you love has gone to sleep
Memories, clothes, ornaments, books and cd/records/tapes
Children too, if blessed in that way
But they have gone
And apart from those visible and mental remainders
It seems they were never here.
It's difficult to explain how the brain unravels all that information
You stare at they're seat (where are they, why aren't they here?)
You stare at their bed
You ask why aren't they using they're stereo?
Reading their books?
Were they ever really here?
Your brain
Your heart tells you they were
That they filled your life
Their love warmed
Their caring often healing.
Yet their absence seems unintelligible.
Your tears wash your eyes
Missing that now apparently never-person
But they are not a never-person
They are your icon
Your beacon
The flame in your heart
But part of you says how cruel is love/life

That it can dismember their and yours relationship
It takes them
And you then again sometimes at your lowest ebb
That it has all been a figment of your imagination.
I miss my Gaynor
And stare around at this 'New World'
A world that feels as though it is a dream
That I never wake from.
Cruel, cruel life.

12/10/24

Wonder

I don't need to witness a solar eclipse to find wonder
I don't need to see the Aurora Borealis to know beauty
I only have to think and ponder upon life with my darling Gaynor
And that is enough beauty and wonder to fill a trillion lifetimes.

11/10/24

Fairness

Fairness
Obscure your visage
Reveal not further your distasteful juggling
Deeming what is fair or not.
You would ne'r know fairness if it bit your hindquarters
Smiling and offering bouquets as a platitude
You are abominable in your attitude of justice
Fairness, pah!, you are but a pariha and pustules of sores be poured upon you.
Life extinguished at a wave of foppish hand
A handkerchief waved in dismissal when you are questioned
Fairness, you leave a stench in the air
Your indifference proves your uncaring soul.
Be off
Take yourself to the outer reaches of nowhere
Let others deem justice or injustice the fact
For your haphazard selections of lives to be forfeited is abhorrent.
People grieve their loved ones that have been taken
Whilst apparent creatures of worthlessness traverse their ills
Begone fairness, be gone
You have no place in many people's spheres.

30/9/24

Love Story

Every love story is beautiful
Every heart that finds its mate is lucky
A wondrous thing to behold
A heart, and hands to hold.
Every love story is unique
It may be woven at the beginning by human hands
But fate has its way of manipulating human agencies
To contrive the joining of two hearts from separate paths.
Every love story is beautiful, wonderful, a rainbow in golden aspect
Every love story is a story to behold
And the two hearts that are joined
See beautiful lights and feel remarkable rhythms.
Every love story is beautiful...
Appreciate yours to the fullest.

10/10/24

'If' Says A Lot

If
Oh such powerful words
So small
Little on letters
But...
But the power contained in it
If...
IF
What words of hope lay behind the saying
What words of longing
What emotional hopes and dreams lie within that short statement
The tears of sadness that drip into the word.
If
If the world would such or such
If he/she would only see how much I love them
If only he/she had not fallen ill
If they had not fallen asleep
If I could hold, hug and hear their words.
If
IF.
Often those two letters hide such huge sadness and heartbreak
And occasionally just that word
The look in the speaker's eyes
The way it was phrased
Finishes the sentence.

6/10/24

Spellbound

Conjuring
Drawing designs in the air
Words indistinct
Coloured lights
Spheres floating high and low
Fingers moving slowly, carefully
Manifestations
Music of voices fill the room
This is magical
Magic...
With these spells the Magi works to find love
To find his soulmate.

You and me
We needed no such paraphernalia
No such arts
For fate guided us into each others path
Your journey if altered by one step
Mine too, had my steps not kept to the path laid before me
Then our conjoining would have missed
Missed by miles
Our steps taken us where
I know not
Nor do I wish to.

Though our life had such a sad, sad heartbreaking finale
You my love going to sleep
Cursed for some reason
By a cruel, twisted anomaly
And I uter oaths daily for that
Hurl abuse at the cosmos
And cry...
Our life other than that
Needed no spells and conjuring
For our love was
NATURAL MAGIC

28/9/24

It Is Tender

It is tender upon the bleeding heart
That the darkling sky surrenders not
To the advancing sun attired in its burning shield of gold.
It is tender upon the crying heart
That the sea absorbs the sorrow complete
And never to cast tears beneath a lost lover's feet.

1997

Little Dormouse

The Dormouse snuggled into her nest
Burrowing into her warm bedding
Yawning she said "I am so very tired"
Closed her eyes and drifted gently to sleep.
Little Dormouse never woke up
Her weakened body surrendering to the dark
Her illness too much
Even though she was sad
It was for the best
That she found her rest.

Everyone who loved brave, beautiful little Dormouse cried
For she was and is greatly loved and missed
Again her lovely face never to be kissed
Her little hands not to be held.
Whale thinks on his beautiful love daily
His tears are his token to his sleeping love
The days are empty now of her playfulness
Her gentle nature and kindness.
Whale sits daily...
Lost
Drifting through the now hollow hours
Knowing his Dormouse in the magic land
Is surrounded by all kinds of creatures and flowers.
Come nighttime my sweet
Sleep tight in your gold and silver rose
For those hours in Tir nA nOg offer a beautiful repose.

17/9/24

There Is A Song

There is a song I hear my darling
Whether in wind, rain, snow or sun
I hear it in my heart my love
Before barely it has begun.
There is a song I hear my beloved
Whether daytime or night
I hear it in my body my love
And hold my body tight.
There is a song
Sung from your sweet lips
It tingles my soul my love
Sparking my fingertips.
The song is you adored one
That I miss so very much
And when I think of you my sweet
I feel your gentle touch.

29/8/24

No Box of Chocolates

Forrest Gump
You were completely wrong
Life is not a box of chocolates
The filling is on the inner lid or sheet insert
Life...
Is a lottery
You get your ticket when you are born
And the years unravel the prizes you receive.
Some people get Wonka's Golden ticket
Others a mediocre life
And others...
The barrel of fetid, rotten fish innards
A life spanning a hundred years or more
Some taken barely out of the womb
Quite a few people have minor ills
Others life changing or ending injuries or disease.
A few find their lifetime love first time
Some after a couple of toe dips in the water
Some never find love and make their journey alone
Never tasting once the bittersweet taste of love
Bitter because it ends in acrimony
Sweet because it is almost perfection
My last love, my lost love
Was the love of my life.
Sadly disease took her away from her family and myself
And that is the bittersweet of my love story

The sweetness of our love
The bitter taste of tears and sorrow when she went to sleep
So those who are lucky to be wrapped in the comfy blanket of love
Do not take for granted
For one day it is there
Another.... Gone.
Like a cold wind leaving you shaking
Within your own individual nuclear winter.

24/8/24

Dreams

Follow me into my dreams
As long as I sleep undisturbed long enough
And your sleep is deep and gentle.
I find lockers that when opened contain rooms
I step into them and people appear
I hear them and someone says she is Gaynor
But bears no semblance
I see colours on walls
Pitch patches of primary
Specks and splashes of secondary
Then they mingle.
I find myself out of the locker and in another room
I'm walking with a lady but I don't hear her speak
I don't know who
But she knows me.
Then I'm somewhere outside
High and monochrome
I hear animals
I see dogs, cats, all sorts of creatures
But when I see a human I do not know them.
Then I wake
I know that somewhere unremembered in the dreams
I did find Gaynor
I sense it
But not allowed to remember.
I suppose that when I do remember
It will be my journey's end
And we are together again.

15/8/24

Dreams #2

Who do we walk with in dreams?
I would say they are those we love and lost
For often when I wake from a dream
I feel as if I've been hugged
Held in warm, loving, gentle arms.
Of course there are nightmares
Something in the day has twisted our syntax/cortex
And it is trying, like a toilet, to flush the waste away
Disquieting and dark
Very odd and Dali-esque.
Those nice and gentle dreams
Even flying with the birds
Is the elation of being with those that care for us
And our sleeping body and mind celebrates
Rejoices at the dream-time union.
Who do we walk with in our sleep?
That make us calm and relaxed when we wake
They are our loved ones
And they be our 'Angels'.

16/8/24

A Little Poem

Speaking to you with no replies
Brings echoing tears to my eyes
My voice not silent in this air
Your voice so silent your voice so fair.
Looking for you in the light
Looking for you in my sleep at night
Not holding you here oh my dear
At night in dreams I hold you near.
Life does bring eddies and cataracts that is true
Life a storm of sadness without you
Whirled by emotions every day
Tossed and thrown every which way.
A leaf in hurricanes is how It feels
Manic dancing of Scottish reels
The world my love is topsy turvy
A crumbling mountain from which to survey.
So this little work of little worth
From out my heart was given birth
For you my dearest I miss so much
And yours my love, is the gentlest touch.

12/10/23

Dance Time

It never ceases to move me
Amaze me
Strictly playing for you
A tribute to our love
As I've said before
You 'Loved, loved it
So I record it to watch the next morning
Knowing you will be sitting in your seat
Feeling inside the warning
That it will upset me
But let that be the beautiful price of love.
The Fleckles instigate trickles
Jive brings more
Waltzes, Foxtrots, Sambas and Two-step.
I cannot watch without deep emotion
The sad emptiness of my arms
Whilst the dancers connect physically
Tears, yes on my living room floor
I watch and sorrow
A small price to pay
For the pleasure the program gave you
And I know, still does.
My partner in love, in dance
Our deep romance

And though we never danced together
She'll be forever
My DANCING PARTNER.
Gaynor, the Terpsichorean Dormouse.

8/10/23

Tender Is The Touch

Tender is the velvet touch
I miss so much
Loving and gentle the kiss
That I so, so miss
Warm and loving the one that sat with me
And I tire so much without the face I long to see
Beloved to the universe's edge is the one I adore
Longing, longing for that welcoming, open door
Tender, loving, gentle and warm is the one
That is today and will always be my song..

6/10/23

Final Breath

Fear not the final breath
It brings peace
It takes you to those you love and lost
It relaxes stress
Smoothes creased and pained faces
Eases sorrow.
Fear not the final breath
In some ways it is a friend
Takes you to velvet sweetness
Soothing rest
Then hands reach and arms enfold
The final breath is warm, not cold.

29/9/23

Buttercup

The golden yellow of the buttercup
Is reflected in your smile
The warm golden yellow
Mirrors the warmth of your heart
It blooms
Hiding itself amongst tall grass or taller blooms
As you kept yourself shielding from stares or gazes
The buttercup though vibrant and beautiful
Is unassuming
As you were my beautiful Lady.
Not everyone needs to be a rose or an orchid
Demanding in their looks that others LOOK at them
Your beauty was obvious to those who looked
But you were unpretentious
Mild
Glowing in your way in the way you wished
Inside
Beautiful as the outside
Warm as the outward smile.
A delightful, amusing, intelligent, kind, generous, caring soul.
Bless you
You adorned the life of your family and myself
And most definitely should have basked in the sun
Lived a longer life than you did.
You my Dormouse, my Buttercup Dormouse.

23/10/23

Will You

Will you take my hand?
And wander free
Will you not show me this place's delights?
Will you not share them with me?
The clear sparkling waters
The mountains purple topped with snow
Will you not show me the treasures?
That make you shine and glow.
Will you not let me taste?
The fruit of this land
We'll wander free forever
If you take me by the hand.
Will you not place a kiss upon my cheek?
And say my name as sweet as you can
For I can not bide after dawn
With you in this land.
Will you not take my hand?
And bid me to stay
But you say to me Dear Whaley
Today is not the day.
Will you come again in the night?
Take my hand to wander this place
And let me hold and look upon you
And your beautiful face.

Will you tell me when 'tis the day?
When I can be at peace and rest
Will you tell me when I can stay?
To be with my truest and best.

21/9/23

Days of Promise

Days of promise
Nights of expectation
But those days became soiled
The nights emptied of all magic.
The promise of days of light
Laughter, conversation
Excursions and the sweet sweet bond
Of love and deep-seated friendship
Rolling on
Now and after
Became dark and chilled
The nights of magic
Knowing that the gift
Gaynor's presence
Was an empty parcel
Crumpled in a corner.
No days of promise
Only expectations of a nothingness
No nights of magic
The spell withdrawn.
So much of the day is void
Silent of a certain voice
The presence of the special one
A cloud that refuses to lift except for odd minutes.
Days of promise
Nights of magic

I beg of you
Make the most of every parsecond
Any moment you can steal from something else
For one day those days and nights are expelled
Become chill, empty air.
Days of promise
Nights of magic
To lose them my friends
Is Shakespeare at his most tragic.

16/9/23

Flowers and Butterflies

Flower petals floating upon the breeze
Partner dancing butterflies
Pinks, blues, yellows, greens and perfect whites
Adorn the cloud spotted turquoise skies
Flowers
Butterflies
Symbols of you
So beautiful
So tender and true
Your hands tended my wounds and hurts
With the touch of satin softness
The gentleness of butterfly wings
Flowers of love you bestowed
Upon loved ones
Your inner light glowed.
Petals
Butterflies
The colours and softness
The graces of you.

16/9/23

Walk With Me

Walk with me my love
Talk with me my dear
I travel with you daily
I talk to you to keep you near
Walk with me my beloved
Whether sun or rain
Walk and talk with me
Again and again.
I walked with you days past
Talked daily and laughed
We walked and talked
Travelled the same path.
Walk with me my sweetheart
Talk or whisper in my ear
For I travel with you daily
And long to hold you near.
I do not see you my love
When I traverse the days
I fail to hear your voice
And the sadness inside me lays.
Walk with me my Gaynor
Talk to me gentle and kind
Take my hand in yours my love
Ease my grieving mind.

I long to walk with you my dearest
I long to speak with you again
Travel with me my life's love
My best and truest friend.

10/9/23

The Frontier

Space
The 'Eternal' Frontier
A rocket would travel lightyears upon lightyears
Never reaching the end
That space, that void is much like loss of a loved one.
That place, that gap, almost feels eternal to the heart
It has no edge, only a core
That core is the loved one
Their memory which is deeply embedded in your soul
Lives within you.
That being said
They are missing in physicality
Their being
Their ethereal presence surrounds you
Cloaks and embraces you.
And that being said too
Their absence is deeply gouged
Your personal, bleeding, aching Grand Canyon
Their love warms the space within that they're passing brought
BUT SADNESS REFUSES TO LEAVE THAT SPOT.

It too can be and often is, immeasurable.
It has no lifespan
No eggtimer for sands to cease trickling
No ticking clock that will ring an alarm to bring it to an end
It has its own timespan.

And it will cease one day
And maybe that day will be the one in which, you too pass
Leaving canyons in others hearts.

31/8/23

Your Gift

My darling
Whether it is a short or longer time
Before we are together again
The ribbons of love that tie us as one
Will without wear or strain
Be our bridge of emotions.
My beloved
This man will be as good a man as he can
To encompass your gleaming facets
Hold your life's memory strong
Surrounded by castle battlements of adoration
These walls will not be breached.
My Gaynor
The man in this place daily weeps
Missing so much the lady he held
The lady he beheld
That he longs again to cast his eyes upon
And embrace her in his arms.
Lady Gaynor
Not one million stars could outshine your light
Not one million gifts at my feet
Be of more worth than the gifts you gave me
Your love, presence, faith, humour and intelligence
All encompassed in the one person…
You my love, my Lady, my Gaynor.
That's My Darling

Gifts of Love, Treasures of Life

That's my darling
There by my side
Holding my hand
I'm glowing inside
That's my darling
Reflected in my eyes
How could I not love her
If I didn't that would be a surprise
That's my darling
Carried within my heart
And she's been there
Right from the very start
That's my darling
Painted upon my days
And she'll be there
Today, tomorrow, always
That's my darling Gaynor
Who I miss so very much
And it hurts my soul
We can no longer touch
That's my darling Gaynor
My sun, my stars and moon
I will sing her lovesong
In every style of tune
That's my beloved darling
And will be until the seas run dry
Until the days wind down
Beyond the time I bid the world goodbye.

24/8/23

I Would Kneel

I fall to my knees at your feet
Well, I would if I could and you were here
I prostrate myself at your memory
Embrace the air in which you talked
Kiss the floors upon which you walked
Look out at the stars in wonder
Gaze at the moon that you loved so much
Often it was your companion when sleepless
Your curtain open just a touch
To observe its passage
Before it disappeared from view
Much like I did with you
Observing your journey through years
And now my view obscured by tears
When speaking to your absent person
Looking upon the photographs
Of the stellar image of my Lady.
I prostrate myself at your feet
And would stay there, immobile
Until time takes its toll
And then my Lady Gaynor
I would be able to kneel at your feet
Two souls reunited.

4/8/23

If I Had Arms As Long As Time

I wish I had arms as long as time
For I could hold you my darling mine
From our first days together
Until the end of ever.
If I had arms as long and strong as time
They would manipulate the wish of mine
That I could hug and embrace you
In whichever eon I choose
And my love and arms my beloved
You they would never lose.
Leaping objects arm in arm
Evading all those wicked things
Around the evil 'C' word
We forever run rings.
If I had arms as long as time
And arms huge and strong as steel
I wish for you so many things
And make those things real.
If I had arms as long as time
I would hold you best friend of mine
We'd be forever companions
Walking in love's aura of flame
If I had arms as long as time
We would never be parted again.

3/8/23

The Unicorn

The mists across the landscape
Lay like a thick grey blanket upon a bed
Trees almost primeaval protruded from the summit
Then gradually towards the centre they rippled
A small parting appeared
A white cone protruded
Then before the villagers astonished eyes
A unicorn stepped forward
It spoke, causing the assembled crowd to gasp
"I come to cure the world of it's ills
To bring peace and love amongst all"
One man rushed forward
With axe in hand, cleaved the poor creatures head from it's neck.
The villagers fell upon him
Tearing his clothes
Raining blows upon his head and body
He was dragged to the Lord's castle
And there explained what had occured
The unicorn's blood stained the man
And the Lord had him cast into his deepest dungeon.
Lord DeClare addressed the angry crowd
"My people, I too deplore his actions
No excuse but possibly the fear of witchcraft
We shall never know
It is a very strange occurrence

Let us place the poor creature in a vault
Pay it due reverence for it is myth become fact".
Following his words they proceeded to the place of butchery
But all that remained were blood stains
From which a small tree had sprouted
Upon which a papyrus was attached
These are the words upon it
"THE WORLD IS NOT READY, NOR MAY NEVER BE
FOR WHEN A MIRACLE APPEARS
MANS EYES AND EARS SEEM BLIND AND DEAF
THE CURE FOR DISEASES
THE END TO WAR
BROTHERHOOD SEEMS CAST ASIDE.
IT IS UPON HIS OWN INTELLIGENCE AND ABILITIES
TO BRING PEACE
END DISEASES
I OFFER NO MORE THE GIFT OF PEACEFUL, LONG
LIFE
UPON YOUR HEADS IT IS.

28/7/23

Patterns

Patterns designed by sunlight
Through leaves it glimmers and floats
Dancing shadows upon woodland floors
Silhouettes stand starkly upon whitewashed walls
Drying petrol specked puddles
Premiere their rainbow shows across the surface.
Patterns designed by memories
Through the cinema of the mind
Dancing people laughing, smiling and holding hands
Silhouettes cast by floodlight moonglow
Patterns created by reminiscences
Highlight their pathways within tears.
Patterns
Beautiful
Happy
Sad
Lost in the whirling world
But gathered
Held dear
Treasured and not to be lost memories.

15/7/23

Featherlight

Featherlight
Touches occasionally upon head
So soft
Almost unnoticeable
But the same place
Every time
The sweet spot
And I know you've gifted me your love
The only way you can
But beloved
I cry silent, gentle tears
Grateful you can still share it.
Featherlight
Yet so exhilarating within me
So warming
Almost unnoticeable
But it ripples my veins
Every time
The sweet spots
And I know again you've touched my heart
The only way you can
But adored one
I cry silent, gentle tears
Grateful you can still bestow it.

25/6/23

Words of Love

Words of love
Spoken so quietly
Soft notes of flute accompaniment
Drift and float
Clouds playing pass the parcel
Message on the way.
Words of love
So gentle and wistful
Birds fly with love notes in beaks
Knowing deeply and keenly
Words of truth I speak
And nest them with down and feathers.
Words of love
Will not stay unspoken
Will not gather dust in my heart
My emotions will not let me rest
I have to pour those words out
From the depths of my breast.
Words of love
So white and pure
Want to be released from inside
The soul of me wants to have its say
Words I wish to tell you my beloved Gaynor
Must sally forth and have their day.

The Master Magician

The 'Master Magician' plays his music
The long notes tingle and bring smiles
The short notes, still as beautiful
Cause tears to welle l
They touch deeply our emotions
But that is the magic
They are our emotions.
His fingers stroke the buttons
As he expands and closes his accordion
The expanded, ribbed instrument
Cast our minds back
The more he expands the sound
The further back our memories travel
And as it compresses
Our minds come forward
Bringing intermingled with smiles, tears
For some will have lost a loved one...
No, everyone will have lost someone
Within the recent times.
His music is supreme
Drifting oceans of colour
The notes occasionally falling as conversations
That trickle to mind.
The 'Master Magician' looks out into the audience
And also feels their joy or sadness
He, after all has his own feelings

And knows loss and happiness
He plays, he cries
He smiles
The lights grow dim
And he's gone.

11/2/23

The Waters

There are waters that flow
And will as long as this earth remains
It's not the seas or rivers
The skies falling rains
For it comes from somewhere magical
The Wellspring of Life
These waters are tears
Of joy
Of grief
Life gives great love
But takes like a thief
The wellspring of the heart will never dry
Will never alter its true course
As long as it is honest and faithful.
These waters are mystical
Effervescent but only reveal themselves
When the source of their being
Leaks from the soul's window
The Wellspring of Life
A secret that each on earth drinks from
And as a reward for that blessing
Our emotions will, whether you like or not
Be visible
So be human
Hide not by fake ideals of masculinity
But show your heart

Wear it upon your sleeve
Tears of happiness when overjoyed
Tears of sorrow when you grieve
Repay that debt for your hearts beating
The Wellspring of Life
Your benefactor.

10/9/22

The Cave of Broken Hearts

Beyond
Beneath
Above
Near
Floating emotions shimmer
Icicles from frozen tears
Hang from ceilings of cold sky
Wherever they form
Their destination is the Cave of Broken Hearts
And therein they will fall
Crash silently to the earthen floor
Shattering and splintering
The icicles thaw
And as they trickle down the paths incline
A faint ethereal sound
Almost flute like
Accompanies the tears
As they meet and drip into the pool.
Scratched illustrations upon the walls
Glow faintly, gilden and silvered
The pictures thereof
Are of Magi from lost peoples
That took upon themselves

The sadness and sorrows of their tribe
And the cave's interior was carved out
As the Palace of Solace
And to this day
The sorrowful tears of the world find themselves here
To be absorbed by the souls of the sleeping Magi.

15/6/22

The Shipwrecks

The ship sailed

Waters calm

Blue sky

The wind filling the sails

A bountiful trade wind

But on the horizon skies darkened

Steel grey and ominous

Gradually they drew closer

Tearing open the small dainty white fluffs

Rain, heavy, torrential

Descended upon the gallant vessel

Throwing it with heaving, immense gales

Off course

And towards rocks

Hidden but appearing to rise from the depths

Dragon toothed sharp

They gouged and ripped

The hull holed

Water pouring into the bulwarks

Yells of the crew unheard

For the maelstrom was godlike.

The ship very slowly

Sinking

Hardly noticeable with human eye
Its descent would be interminable...
Thus, this man describes the voyage.
His Port of Life...
His love, was lost
A tsunami of disease
Feeling the tug of the threat
She could not overcome
His, a broken, tattered heart.
Without her, his love at his side
He is again, shipwrecked
And awaits his final descent
Where he will again reunite
With his beloved
Upon gentle land
And blue skies.

Insidious Creature

Forsooth
Fevers of ague
Seem to be a constant
But verily
It is nought but tremors of darting pangs
It is nought I say
But in truth
It is all
The pangs and sorrow of loss
My companion
Wherewith my companion
My love and sweetheart was truly you.
Dragontooth of life's haphazard dance
Skipping
And as it goes along its merry way
In its midst
The lottery of an uncaring selection process
Attired in garb of hunchbacked jester
Pointing the gaily adorned bladder
And within its core
The poison that instills itself
Taking strength, lightness of step
Happiness and then…
Life itself.
Forsooth
That mean visaged creature

Carries within itself no joy
And unleashes that which crumbles and decays
The joy that love has borne between humanity
The love and adoration that one feels for their beloved.
Monster
What a boon to the universe if thou were vanquished
Removing you in all your forms
Disease, war, pestilence and famine
And also extinguish the face of hate
The mistrust of multifaceted religious inclinations
That humankind sprinkles.
Verily my heart does bleed
But it pours the more for my Lady
As do my eyes.

28/11/21

Love Sweet, Love sour

Oh love
Sweet sprite
Honey of life
You quench, then sustain
But when you depart
Oh the pain
The fractures of the heart.
Often it is incompatibllity that steps in
But then it is mortality
That ungovernable sin
Causes the rupture most profane
That becomes the nemesis.
Oh love
Soothing when in hold
But dreadfully impersonal
When there is a touch of cold
For the loved one
Is taken
Beyond that mysterious veil
Leaving the grieving and bereft
Lost and beyond the pale
Unable to see light for the darkness
That descends upon the senses
The remaining, lonely one
Can summon no defenses
And just suffers the ongoing trauma

Never sure of whether living is the course
Alternative there is
But is such a bitter sauce.

29/11//21

Cost of Some Childhoods

Bruises
Breaks
Beatings
Starvation
A hit list
And again and again
As often as a blow lands
Mistakes by Authorities
Set up to protect
These poor little children
Yet, they were failed
And paid the price
With their lives.
How many...
HOW MANY MORE
CHILDREN
HOW MANY MORE
FAILURES.

3/12/21

Washing Waters

Arrogantly the waters roil
Spume does boil
Currents carry away detritus
They say wash in the waters
Cast away your hurts
Rinse away the dirt of life
But it is impossible
To lose the scars of sadness.

3/12/21

Forever

Forever love
Forever friend
Forever my light
Forever my fantasies flight
Forever my darling
Forever my beloved
Forever adored
Forever much, much more
Forever in my words
Forever in my mind
Forever in my heart
Forever together though at present apart
Forever
I mean forever
Not the moon dimming her beam
Behind diaphanous clouds
Or refusing to glow
Forever, today, tomorrow by the trillion
Forever. I mean come high water or hell
When the sun switches out its nuclear light
Or when the universe rings the final bell
Forever
Even though it's beyond belief
Past the time turns off its timer
And cosmos dust is all that remains
I will be within that dust

Swirling with you
Forever...
Forever
And that I swear.
You my love eternal
Eternally my love.

19/12/21

How Dry The Seas Are

How dry the seas are
Once the rain stops falling
When the sun works its worst
And the tides are Saharan in aspect.
How dry the seas are
When your love is no longer there
When the watering gift of their eyes are closed
When their mouth is silent.
How dry the seas are
When they have passed
Leaving you adrift on immense dunes
And the world seems to cease turning.
How dry the seas are
And seeming never to liquify again
You are left stranded upon the gritty sand
A dehydrated husk of what you were.

18/1/22

To Be Here With Dormouse

Oh to be here with Dormouse
With spring upon her way
With the explosion of flora
Colours to enhance her day.
Oh to be here with Dormouse
The exuberance of her spirit
As the days blossomed
And she would drape herself in it.
Oh to be here with Dormouse
My heart and soul would revel
And laughter conjoined from our depths
Would ring as the sweetest faery bell.
Oh to be here with Dormouse
No more do I need to write
For the sadness of being without her
Does squeeze my heart so tight.

25/1/22

The Seasons

Seasons move upon us
Continuing their cycle
Uncaring of human matters
The tragedies, disasters
Arguments and wars.
Seasons do not notice the tears of sadness
A few more drops of moisture
That adds to what falls from the sky
The sorrow another storm without lightning.
Seasons discount the faltering footsteps
Of one who is aging
For the seasons renew their earthly reign
But humanity visits once, never to return.
Thus the seasons are oblivious of what it is to feel
Our emotional soft underbelly is the price we pay
To be human and suffer loss and grief
The price though dear, is fair.
The seasons know not what joy is
To feel the loving look in a partner's eyes
The warm touch of a gentle hand
The sweet liquidity of a deep kiss
That, humanity would miss.
The seasons move onward
And when we pass and turn to dust, as we must
The seasons will carry our remains for eternity
Then, nature, the seasons and humanity will become one.

29/1/22

Oh! Muse

Oh! muse
Though you sleepeth deep
My heart and soul dost though inspire
And though your silence maketh me weep
Sorceress like you still weaveth your spell
Inspiring multitudes of words to fall
Tinkling like silver bells in crystal water
My very being scored upon time as prose
Though whither are of value or ragamuffin
Tis' others to state the fact.
Oh! muse
Love that I wouldst gather and enfold
Place kisses of sweetest honey
Defend thee to mineown utmost
From ill and threatening people
From chilliest storms of winter
The rays of scorching sun
I wouldst, but feign be life to thee
For sickness foul and cruel
Took you from thy family and I
And in truth
Instead of you, I would have stood your poison
Slept your sleep
For you to dance more steps

Upon this ground.
My muse
I adore thee
Worship thee
And eternally your knight.

31/1/22

Empty Spaces?

These spaces I perceive to be empty
That are according to my eyes
Are full of emotions
Memories waltz and pirouette
Conversations inaudible to all but me
Daily leave my face wet.
Not empty, not vacant and lost
But full of joyous moments
Of happy minutes and hours
That when closing my eyes
I relive again and again
Time doesn't stop but flies.
Not empty spaces
But are jam-packed with love.

9/2/22

Gifts of Love, Treasures of Life

Love Conquers

Love conquers all
Except that of human frailties
Of life itself being conquered
Sickness, violence and heart tiring
Love's physical actions cease
But the glow
The warmth
The affection
Continues
Long after those that gifted
And received its bloom
It transcends the final goodbye
For it is carried in the air
In the kisses felt by the wind
The hands held also embrace the cosmos.
Love conquers all in the purist state of atoms
It moves through the universe
Encircling far off planets
It is of the cosmos
For we came from the depths of far off night
And love was the gift bestowed upon us
In our maturing from the amoeba
To humankind
And love is the gift that we bestow.
And I am privileged to have been allowed to love
And be loved by the sweet Lady Gaynor.

14/2/22

Winds

The wuthering, withering wind
Of age blows upon all
Gusting away childhood
Teen years a whoosh of hormonal confusion
Leading to adulthood
A head on contusion
And often we are unprepared.
We find dalliances
Some apparently THE ONE
But life has other mountains to climb
Playing Kiss Chase and Postman's Knock
Leaving emotions quivering and in shock
But one day
Down a road unexpected
WHAM!
THE ONE
From direction and situation one couldn't have suspected
To reveal a love so strong
Golden
Warm
Special
And sadly short-lived.
The withering, wuthering wind blew again
Leaving one dazed
Grieving and half crazed
Eyes blurred not by age but tears

Shedding more than all the combined previous years.
Withering, wuthering winds
Phantom but make their presence felt.
Be prepared to love as deep as an ocean
But also be prepared to grieve
No seeming end to that emotion.

5/3/22

When The Garden Blooms For Dormouse

The garden will bloom for Dormouse
When the Gardner comes and tends
But Whale will not go out and sit
In case he falls again and never mends
But the main thing are the flowers
For Dormouse to see
When she visits in spirit
That's the important thing to me
The garden is a memorial for Gaynor
For the lady is residing in my heart
And to keep the garden reflecting her beauty
Is to me the important part
Gaynor's Garden of delights
When the Gardner's done her bit
So when Gaynor in spirit visits
My spirit will go out to sit.

7/3/22

Menu of Meaning

Billows and pillows of soft downy touches
Sparkles and glittering of tingly memories
Wafts and draughts of cheeks kissy kissed
And silent silences of words so much missed.
Long misty evenings of bewildered being
Short gasped intakes breathed and replenished
Starved and hungry no morsels adequate
In this island of sadness and famished.
Wispy and tentacled the nighttime air
Chilled and winterly waspish
This banquet of life a crowded miasma
Only offering a dented platter of an unpalatable dish.
Billows and pillows
Streams, currents and cataracts
That whirl upon vagabond moments
A long itinerary, an encyclopedia of facts.

19/3/22

Tis' There

Tis' there by silver'd waters
That runs midst the Forest of Aecamalea
Which bears the sweetest fruit
Where you wander and survey the misty hills
Tis' there that you bide
Telling the faery folk
Of the love you left behind
And he sits here daily
With you stepping gently through his mind.
Tis' there that you sojourn
And learn of Tir Na Nog
Awaiting the time of his calling
And you will offer your hand to guide him
Then again you will be one
Your love united, hearts entwined
That will forever share the sunlight
And he falls asleep so gratefully
To share with you a few short hours of night.
For his nocturnal passage
Allows his spirit for a wee time
To walk the paths to your flowery bed
Where he with you, will lay his head
And will hold you close
Placing gentle kisses on your face
But come the rising sun
Will have to return to his physical place

For that short gift of sharing, its time has run.
Tis' there you pass your days
And here he passes his
Awaiting the night so again he can lay
Cuddled and holding warm
The love that he misses
On awakening every dawn.

24/3/22

Just Like Galadriel

Just like Galadriel
She rises with the sun
Telling me of her new existence
As one of the ever young
Saying that in time
I too will be so blessed
And not to fret at her sleep
That I need to rest
Seek peace of mind.
She brings flowers too at dawn
Then again, flowers from the sun
To glow through the dark hours
To know her love shines upon me
And forever will.
Just like Galadriel
She has that faery magic
Cooling my brow when I feel pain
And leaving within me
That eternal spark
That helps me through the night
Her arms holding tight the love
We shared
Showing too how much she cares.
She, the Lady of Golden Sunbeam
My beloved Gaynor.

26/3/22

House of Shared Emotion

The walls are lonely for lack of her
The lampshades shed tears
Resembling crystal chandeliers
And I know I'm not alone
When I cry in my bed
For I hear the entire house
All its contents speaking of their sadness in my head.
The windows stare blankly outward
Reflecting my non inclusive mood
And occasionally not wanting to speak to anyone
Hoping they don't think me rude
But this house and sole occupant
Share their sadness and their grief
At the truth of my far distant words
That time is no ordinary thief.
The walls don't absorb her words now
Or her gentle laughter
And the carpets seemed to have absorbed every ripple
Every echo of every sound
And I sit moping and glassy eyed
Like a disinherited hound
Who whipped not by cruel hands
But by the turn of Fate's cards.
The house in its silent brick

Utters not one sentence of complaint
But I know from the aura
That it too shares the combined emotions
Of every piece of furniture
Ornament, clothing, and appliance....
They too miss you as I do.

26/3/22

Timestreams

Drifting along timestreams of memory
Feeling the love
Seeing the sun
Drinking up your company
You, my beautiful cup of tea
But drifting those lines past
I feel the chill blow across my bow
Jolting me forward
To the here and now
Oh my love
If I could bottle your voice
Uncork at times my spirit falters
Put your hologram in the room
There again it would not give your warmth
A shallow representation of you
But your voice
Your smile
I wish that they could be audible and visible.
Timestreams cause me heartache
And feeling more empty.

5/4/22

We Are All Children

We are all children when we cry
Fingers grasping for something
Soft to snuggle ourselves into from long past days
Or something hard to inflict a pain
In retaliation for being hurt
Hurt by physical impact
Or emotional bombardment.
We are all children when we cry
Curling into a ball
Trying to refit ourselves back into a womb
Wanting the safety of a special place
Seeking the protection of our birth mother
Or we run and hide into a place apart from others
For some are embarrassed by the tears they weep.
We are all children…
At some time when we are adults
There is a time we revert back
Then we become children
We should not be embarrassed
For tears are part and parcel of life's journey
We should accept that.
WE ARE ALL CHILDREN.

8/4/22

Time Runs Forever

Time runs forever
But never grows tired
It is we that tire and falter
And time brings about its climax
Then we close our eyes
That, the most basic of facts.
Time runs forever
Until the universal climax
Then time hits the proverbial wall
Collapsing into the nothingness
Then too it closes its symbolic eyes
And along with everything, forever rests.
Though in a paradox
Time in some way will continue
For what can stop the ever onward beat
Even of nonexistence
For time is uncountable
And held not to account.

14/4/22

More Than Love

More than love
How to express it
Impossible
All you can do is skim
Touch the surface.
The butterflies as love begins to bloom
The itchy longing to see each other again
The lightheadedness at the first kiss
Then love takes root
Friends given the boot
For every available minute you want to spend with the other.
It deepens
The hollow feeling at a slight argument
The volcano inside when you make up
A small gift to make amends
For now this love is also your best of friends.
A love That was more than a love
A love that is your life
The world
The cosmos
And to express in words
Spoken or written...
Impossible.
The only way to put it to you
Is you'll have to wait
Wait until you feel that expansive swelling of the chest

The warm glow of golden cinders.
But be advised
When the one you love so strong is taken
Health causes that void
Or old age
The cold, emptiness you feel
Your soul now in a cage
Unable to touch
To converse
With that Be All
That was your soulmate.

WE LOVED WITH A LOVE THAT WAS MORE THAN LOVE.

19/4/22

Stardust and Moonglow

Falls of stardust
Sparkle upon your footprints
Moonglow lights upon your memory
Sunshine blazes in all you did
The world turns
Forever within your sphere
For you are you
And irreplaceable my dear.
My heart beats incessantly
For love of you
It too glows with adoration
Adding rainbows to the darkest hue
My memory
Forever imprinted with your specialness
But if I put it simply
You were and are the best.
I feel so humble
You took and held my hand
People that never knew you
Will never understand
You left a mark upon all
That got to know you my love
And all the things you were
Glow from above.

12/5/22

I Flicker

I flicker like a shadow
In and out of today and the past
Looking for traces of you
Wanting to relive our time together.
I flicker in and out of shadows
The light blinding in its honesty
The dark unforgiving in its harsh brutality
Both imaging the facts.
I flicker like a shadow
Feeling unsubstantial and open
The warmth doesn't warm
The cold a permanent coating.
I flicker
I shift
My body breaking up like a poorly stored video
Waiting for the tape to snap.
I flicker
Flicker and fade.

19/5/22

In The Velveteen Stream

The endless stream stretches to the stars
Your fingers reaching to touch their glow
And as you drift through the velveteen expanse
Your skin is tingled by moondust
An occasional comet bids hello as it illuminates your path
Leaving the fiery trail you must follow.
As you travel
Music fills your ears
Unwritten symphonic masterpieces hummed by the cosmos
And a voice enters your mind
The voice you long for
The voice of your lost love.
In far off galaxies
Silver ice gems twinkle
Winking their knowing eyes
Knowing the secret of secrets
That only the final sleep surrenders to the sleeper
And you travel onward, outward.
Planets loom now
But some still not visible to your eyes
And the music continues
Almost a synthesized poem by Bach and Tangerine Dream
You feel the presence of your loved one approach
And in your sleep, you smile.

28/5/22

Gifts of Love, Treasures of Life

The Reel of Film

Your life over too soon
Like a cinema film reel
Tearing
The movie already viewed spinning on its reel
The part left to view
Trapped and unmoving in the feeder mechanism
But it isn't a movie
It's real life
Yours ended and the curtains brought down
Whilst others view the blank screen
Missing you
Missing you.
Flickering images replay
A morning picture show
An afternoon matinee
And an evening performance
All around sound of a silent film
And I sit
An audience of one,
As if watching the saddest, most moving film ever
And I eventually retire to bed
Worn out
Sad
Missing you
Missing you
And the flickering images still playing through in my mind.

19/2/25

This is going to be quite short, succinct
And I'm not usually like that with my writing but...

When I think of all of Gaynor's characteristics
All of her tremendous lust for life
The light she brought
The love she gave and had in abundance
I can only say this
That men never, ever think there is such a lady on earth
That they don't exist
And for some reason, some whim of fate
This magnificent lady came into my life.
I was blessed, honoured, privileged and extremely fortunate
For our paths to cross
Our stars of all stars glowed in the same sphere.

I love you my darling. Now and eternally.

24/1/25

Memories

I have no idea what triggers the surges of emotion
The windfall snow and ice of sadness
That already lays deep and packed hard within me
But it causes the day to turn into a polar icepack
A day that will bring no warmth or sunshine
No respite from the withering of sadness inside my heart.
This morning whilst washing
A memory hit me and talk about right field
An oblique stirring for no reason whatever
Of the lift serviceman asking if he could use the toilet
And I had to say no because Gaynor was resting, on the settee
Having had some bad days with her cancer.
I visualised her, eyes closed, gently breathing
Finding at least for a short period
The peace of a gentle slumber
Shutting the blinds upon her hurts
Upon her worries for it was before she was informed of her lifespan
And I wanted nothing to disturb my beloved.
Memories come like flashes of lighting
And often the squall of tears follows
Puddling your insides
Drenching your hours
And it is what it is
For some memories though sadness accompanies them
Are priceless.

Treasured and held deep, deep within the stronghold of ' Fortress Heart '.
My beloved Gaynor
May the flashbacks continue even though they bring sadness
I could not live without them
I am having to live without you here
And to lose them,well, my world would end
Probably too, my life.

4/2/25

Déjà vu

Deja vu
Been here before
And I'm sorry if those reading this
Feel I'm a bit of a bore
And reading my jottings
Is probably getting to be a monumental chore.
But I'm very down
Feeling, again you say, extremely sad
I find these days more often
It would be better for me if I went completely mad
And the days I'm wallowing in
Are not the best I've had.
Love does this to you
When you lose the one you carry in your heart
What do you do?
Where do you start?
When all is grey and dark
Aching for the one from whom sleep has forced you apart.

Deja vu
One does not get used to this
One is always looking around
Looking for the one you miss
Daily seeing nothing but a well of sorrow
Tears leaping the edge of the abyss.
Yes, you are probably tired of my weeping and moaning

And yes, I am too
But every day I'm living this hell
What am I to do?
Except try to purge the poison no matter how little it helps
But maybe a dark place is also an abode for you.

Deja vu
We who grieve are not alone
So all I can say now is...
Bless you and like me, continue to struggle through.

23/1/25.

This House (A short story in prose)

This house tells a story
First chapter of furnishings
Ornaments
Clothing
Put in their places
And afterwards
The two occupants nodding and smiling faces.
Second chapter
You out into garden
Tending
Caring
Putting it more to rights
Then later
Settling down with Whaley and pleasant nights.
Chapter third
My body starting to give problems
And the coming of Rosie dachshund
Lots of fun because she's just bonkers
Not far behind due to more balance and pain
Wheelchair my way in the world
Difficult to process in my brain.
Chapter four
Rosie has health problems
And we cannot afford the cost

So new home and we shed tears as she waves goodbye
We just amble on making the best
Not a lot of money for anything to help lighten the mood
But we deal with it, it is just another test.

Chapter five

Lighting

Storm

You have cancer

You fight like hell

A true Amazon warrior/ gladiator

But oh my darling Gaynor, for you no bell.

Chapter seven

This is shorter

Not much to tell

The grief and sadness

A living hell.

Chapter eight

Yet to be writ

But it won't be much different to the previous chapter
No excitement and very, very little laughter.

9/12/24

Words Of Songs Hit A Chord

'Stand By Me'
Oh that song
The feelings it engenders
The emotions that I feel well deep
Bubbling away and they come forth
Dampness to the eyes
Words 'How I miss you my love, here, standing beside me.
And yes 'When The Night Has come'
And The Moon Is The Only Light'
Those lyrics and I concur with them
I won't be affraid because I know you stand by me
Glowing away inside.
Stand By Me I know you do
And I will always stand by you.

24/11/24

Photographs of You

Your photographs I have placed
To be a presence
Your lovely face
Eyes glimmering
The illuminated pathway to your beautiful soul
And those that knew and met you
Also saw the lady I love and adore
The lady so gentle
Unassuming
Happy to be out of the limelight
But so pleased for others.
Your photographs show traces of the spark
That made you special
The spark that ignited the fuse to fight
Battle that dreaded disease
But accepting so placidly
The words you must have awaited with bated breath
You only had eleven months
Then it was a calming wind
The truth
But you were magnificent.
Your photographs show a light and spark
Though they daily make me cry
For the spark, fire and life-force
Are no longer here
To take my hand

What cruelty
One so loving and beneficent
Is absent from the world
Photographs of Gaynor
My Lady and My Girl.

Where You Reside

Where you reside
By Moonwater Lake
Within the valley of Rainbows
And you sleep
Do you dream of me My Lady
After I have left your side
After our few hours of huggy, cuddly sleeptime.
Where you roam by sparkling streams
And within the palace walls
Do you think of me with love
Missing our companionship
Our conversations and laughter.
I do my love
For I talk to you often
Which brings forth tears
I have never loved before this way
Felt the empty, echoing pangs
The uselessness of Being.
Where you reside
Tasting sun and moon juices
Sweet fruits of all kinds
I too wish to reside
And forever My Lady, My Love
Be at your side.

Gifts of Love, Treasures of Life

Legends

Myths and legends
Oh they are misted
Unicorns
Leprechauns
With their crock of gold
At a rainbow's end
My crock of Golden Sunbeams
Is my beloved and best friend
And I know she is there.
She said to me years ago
"We knew each other in another time
And knew we'd meet again"
We did, and loved
Until the very end…
But not really the end
For love and devotion transcends that veil
And I love her totally and completely
Nobody else could ever do for me.
Legends
No…Gaynor is my legend
Brave as anyone I ever knew
And I seal these words on myths
With a written kiss.

15/1/22

How Big Sadness Is

People meet
And if lucky, fall in love
Love grows
Filling the hearts as a balloon
Then,
Often the unthinkable occurs
One is taken
Sometimes before their time
And the other grieves.
Time passes
People say you should move on
Don't dwell
But why is it
That sorrow doesn't decrease
Like love blooming it too can swell.
I know
For each day
I miss my love more
And I wonder when the time will come
That the sadness becomes larger than my own body
I feel I'm outgrowing my own skin.

Dreams and Actual Reality

The urge sometimes comes
To kiss the cardigan and blanket
The shawl and slippers
That I have left where Gaynor sat
And occasionally her clothes upstairs
Tangible things I can see and touch
To kiss them for the pleasure they gave
To the lady I love so much.
I sit here still casting glances at her seat
And as I watch, using the term loosely
The TV across the room
My eyes often look to her photos
Memories dance in illuminated glory
To a time I could touch and to my love speak
A huge chasm dwells within me
And ease of this grief, unhurriedly seek.
I cannot believe, my brain in part refuses
That the vacancy is permanent
And not just that my beloved is away, visiting
I still await her key in the door
But her purse is near her seat, keys inside
As are other things she often used
Mug, birdwatching binoculars
Others too I cannot remove, to them I am fused.
Reality is the curse from empty seat to purse
Dream, a long one I would wake from

And my darling Gaynor sitting here
I would a torrent of kisses place upon.

Underhanded Cards

There's son 'Son of A Bitch'
Dealing from the bottom of the deck
Using lead weighted dice
In their game of poker and 'craps'
Trying to deal crooked hands
And getting away with the whole shebang.
You were the one given the bad hands
That found your bet blocked
Then the roulette wheel
Grinding out deficient spins
Sinners win
You my poor darling suffered their sins
Loaded against you, I can see clearly
And as I love you dearly
I accuse the Fates for cheating
Handling out their beating
Of short years of true happiness
And those in the viper's nest
Denying the years you deserved
You, ill served
Oh sweet lady
Gambling never your style
And while you smiled
A doppelganger sat in your seat
At the casino of decision
Howls of derision

As you lost hand after hand
Dice rolling as if in sand
Then the invoice laid out before your eyes
Clouding the blue skies
You lost whilst unknowing that games were played
The imposter in your seat
Unfit to sit at your feet
Played in the most lackluster way
And onward drew that day
The final chip laid down
And you closed your eyes
How I despise those disreputable cheats
I'd tie them in chains and sheets
Cast them into Etna's molten core
Slam upon them sunlight's door
To leave them forever in the dark
Never a spark of love they showed
Unlike my darling who glowed
And was denied a fair deal
A fair and honest hand of life
I love you my darling, sweet Gaynor
In all but name, my wife.

It Is Tender (2)

It is tender upon the memory of loved ones sleeping
That our words are scattered wildly
That our words do not fall on undeserving ears
And are not diluted or withered by years.

It is tender upon our world and its future inhabitants
That we become less careless with our treasure
That we sear less the grass and cool the boiling skies
It is tender and it is beneficent that we appreciate what is before our eyes.

It is tender
It is TENDER
IT IS IMPERATIVE.

28/9/24

The Light

In early hours I awake intermittently
Betwixt midnight's toll
And dawns breaking of the yolk of golden sun
I gaze around my dark bedroom
Eyes often sore from weeping the night before
And as I close my eyes to fight my way back into uneven slumber
A pale, dim light appears
I know what it is
The light of love
The light of you
Showing you watch over me
My lighthouse
My beacon.
Bless you a trillion fold my darling
Bless you my Gaynor.
Though this light is behind my shuttered lids
It is there, nightly
As you are
In my waking mind and heart, daily

Betwixt

Betwixt

Betwixt our fingers touching
Is air
Betwixt your smile and my eyes
Is air
But betwixt our love
Is a corridor
One to another
Glowing
But in my being
Is sadness
For missing my beloved is immense
A planet of sorrow.
Betwixt you and me in heart
No space exists
Seeing you is obscured
By timeless ethereal mists.
Betwixt and between
Covered and unseen
Is our gleaming, golden connection
Betwixt thy and I
Deep and loving affection.

How It Is...Is Not As It Was

The heart misses its love daily
The solo, echoing beat sounds a dirge
The empty spaces, reminders of once filled light
Spaces rendered bankrupt of feelings
Trailing thermals of chill sail freely overhead.
I will say this, as bleak as things are
How they always seem to appear
There are times of sun and a smile
I never thought I could surface from the depths
But I have begun to rise above the floor of total desolation.
There is light
There still are shadows
I know there always will be
And no, you will not find yourself as you once were
It is impossible, even if you find love again
That part of you is partitioned from the remainder.
Footsteps will become a few ounces lighter
Laughter will rumble and rise in your throat
Smiles will decorate your face
But deep inside that love that meant the universe
Will reside and remain part of your psyche.
I will not love again
I could not find that warmth, companionship and equilibrium
with another
But that is me

It is not you
And we wear a different coat and shoe.

19/2/25

Mirrors

In the mirror before me
I see a mirror
And it reflects yesterday
And within that mirror
Is also another mirror
Reflecting the same
A previous day's yesterday
And another, yes, another mirror
On and on they go
Shrinking in size so slightly
Until they reach the day of detonation
The day everything I held dear exploded into waves of sadness
And that day's mirror does not reflect an explosion
But my darling asleep
Never to wake.
How I long to stretch my hands
Long, rubber arms reaching beyond that day
To pull the images I adore
My beloved, smiling, being silly and full of life
But I can't
And all I see before me
Images of tomorrows
With mirrors within stretching back
Past the point in which I am now
And I see me
Sadder, unable to raise above the trench

The trench that symbolises the war and battles
Conflicts that I cannot overcome
Because I miss my darling
And am another loser in the blitzkriegs
That life hurls into our path.
Mirrors
Always reflecting back
And oh how those reflections make you bleed inside.

8/5/22

When A Heart Breaks

When a heart breaks
It will never mend
It sits inside you, fractured
For loss of spouse, partner and best friend.
When a heart breaks
Everything seems to cease
Time lays upon your head
And sorrow seems to increase.
When a heart breaks
You wonder how long you can continue
Life around you moves along
But seems to not see you.
So when my heart broke
Like a clock my workings slowed
And once where sunshine shone
Is now dull and shadowed.
Life, existence
Ticking over
A moon wrecked vehicle
An obsolete lunar rover.
When a heart breaks
It breaks
Never healing
Unrepairable.

7/5/22

Gifts of Love, Treasures of Life

Mellow Is The Music.

Playing a cd that you played
My head resting upon the settee back
Left hand, palm up on your seat cushion
And tears.
Gentle sounds of harp, guitar and synth
In the background faint
Birds singing
A horse neighing
Pegasus, free and wild.
Other tracks with flute, soft timpani and drum
Voices in a Celtic verse
And it takes me to the days
Hearing you play it in your room.
Mellow it would be
Mellow it is
But sad I feel.
Music to charm the gentle mouse
No savage beast in her soul
The beast in me
Roars inwardly at your passing
But mellow I become.
Would that I could feel your hand on mine
Sharing the soothing waves
Aural healing
Accompanies the light running hooves
Wind, satin of cooling current

More birdsong
And mellow I remain.
If only I could see you
Sitting, sharing the music
But I know that the tranquility I feel
Is because you are near
Here
Sitting, listening with me.

4/5/22

Winds

Trees blowing gently in the morning
And the same breeze
Blows memories of better days
When you and I walked hand in hand
Now I retrace those steps
In a phantom land
Not feeling your fingers
But when I concentrate
The touch in my heart lingers.
If only winds could reverse time
Oh love of mine
You would be here
Sitting near
And you my dear
I would never let go
Following you like a puppy
Never out of sight
Holding you tight.
If winds…
If.

23/4/22

In Candlelight

In candlelight my eyes flicker
My captive heart never to be released
For my love is deep as ocean blue
The spume and foam of emotions
Splash the land so fair
For my tears echo in Tir nA nOg
And I cannot stem them
It is easier to stop time
Than those drops for loss of my love
For said time will ne'r heal this heart of mine.
The silvered mirror casts illusions
In the dim dancing reflecting light
Arms dark of the night
Wrap around me as if to solace my pain
But nought will ever dull this
Her face bright and golden
Floats across the glass eyed tormentor before me
I reach deeply within
To embrace my adored
And kiss her again.
In candlelight betwixt night and day
I toss in sleep
I see her but she can never stay
Oh beloved
Oh cruel curse
My love drips its course

Along skeins of ether
And I wish it were as warm
As my arms would be
With words of pledge to thee from me.

29/4/22

Begone

Life
You thieving blaggard
Stealing dreams
Hopes
Events
Futures
Enjoyment
Haphazardly hopping, skipping and jumping
Imprinting your size elevens
On people's heads and hearts
Squeezing the juice of sweetness from golden apples
Until you leave a dessicated husk of something resembling a lemon
Pulverising
Pounding
Crushing
Leaving dust
Entrails of loss in your wake.
Begone you damnable disease
Begone
Infect no more
Leave no more tears and faltering, disheveled dreams
You cursed
Maggot riddled embodiment of horror
Let those alone that are here
Those to come

Begone, forthwith
You obscene reeking bum
Go wipe the excrement of your cancer from this world
Begone you manure
Begone.

Oh My Dearest

Oh my dearest
I so wanted us to grow old together
To sit huddled up
When cold weather opened its jaws
And the frozen teeth bit hard
To sit in the park
Watching those younger
Walk hand in hand
As we did did
Two elderly lovebirds
Cooing silently
Seeing the love in each others eyes.
Oh my love
I so wanted to give you so much more
Than I was able to do
But I know you were happy with affection
Caring less for what money could buy
For love needs no purse or coin
Just coffee and cake
Trips on the bus to Kenilworth
But being together
Whether TV watching
Or sharing a meal
Loving each other, the real deal.
Oh my dearest
It is just me

That in the cold or sun
Thinks these thoughts
Travels down memory lane
Wishing you were here to do it again
But oh my dearest
My amazing Lady Gaynor
I wait for the time
When again your hand is in mine
And we walk tree lined paths
Oh my dearest, it is taking so much time.

7/4/22

It Is A Sad House

It is is a sad house
Invisible tears drip down the walls
But there is no damp
For the love that lays deep
Upon the carpets and rugs
Absorbs all that the bricks can weep.
It is a sad house
The sobs silent to me
Soak into the walls
But the paint nor paper peels
Though the house is just a building
The loss of you it feels.
It is a sad house
And its sole living occupant
Shares the sense of void
The loss of one so vibrant and energetic
But now the house is like the occupant
Feeling stagnant and static.

6/4/22

Echoes

Echoes
Splashes of water
Small, gentle, saline
They follow swiftly behind the echoes
Almost hand in hand
And often there are visual flashes
You, sitting near me
Smiling at something on TV
Or at a stupid remark I made (deliberately)
I love your smile
To see your eyes twinkle.
Oh those echoes
Often bring the cold fingered touch
The touch that lonely sadness can bring
Then I close my eyes
Shutting away the concrete factuality
I reach out my hand to your seat
Imagining your fingers touching mine
And they gently fold into each other
A flower of hands
Petals of love.
Echoes
Oh they make me sad
Wishing they didn't
But one cannot choose ones emotional reactions
To memories, no matter how warm they are

I have learnt to live with this
Over the past three years
And even though sadness is my companion
I wouldn't change the emotional/echo symbiotic relationship
For it would lessen the love and affection I have for you
And the thousands of golden hours we had.
You, special lady, are an echo of the truest love and friendship.

29/3/22

Lonely For You

I'm lonely for you my dearest
Placing each day's sadness upon shelves
And can feel them gradually bending
Beneath the weight of sorrows
Wondering quite often now
How long must I face the tomorrows
For though I say I'm trying
And others tell me I'm strong
I know from the amount of crying
They're wrong.
I'm lonely for you my beloved
Wanting to be in your company
And wonder how much longer
How much time for me
For I weaken under my body's ills
And there is nothing to cure
Neither medicine or pills
Only your healing heart will mend
Only your closeness to me
My adored and best friend.
I'm lonely for you love of my life
Want only to be with you
And I tire of people saying
You must, she wouldn't want it another way
But it's me on this awful journey
That has to face each Gaynor empty day

I long to close my eyes
Then open them and see you
I hope you forgive these words
But they speak what is true.
I'm lonely for you my darling
And I feel the weakening of my resolve
Only sleep and awakening next to you
Will the heartbreak be solved
I'm lonely for you my only
I'm lonely for you.

27/3/22

The Record Player

A record player spins
No electricity or battery
Cannot be turned off
It is powered by emotion
And upon the platter
A record
Unable to be removed
Plays all day, every day
It is a record of sadness
Loss and solitude
Not solitude of choice
But of cause
The loss of a love
Passed before time
And deserving of so much more.
The record never skips or sticks
Occasionally crackles
But it's played constantly
Though will never lose the ability to emit
The heartbreak it has recorded upon it.
Around it goes
Second by second
Minute by minute
Hour and day upon year.
The record player will stop one day
Gradually slowing down

David Slater

The needle in the record's groove
Whether at the start, middle or end...
It will stop one day
When too the owner of the record player's heart stops
For then the sound of his grief that has played on and on
Will have ended
For he will be with his lost love
And happy songs will fill the air where they walk
Hand in hand.

13/3/22

Inspirational Woman

Inspirational
By the bucket load
Showed me a path to happiness
A truly memorable road
Full of laughter
Coffee and cake
Days out
Coffee and cake
Intelligent conversations
And...ahem...coffee and cake
And when I did something silly or clumsy
I'd hear "SAKE"
And we'd both laugh
Yours delicate
Mine like an emptying bath.
Then when you became ill
Diagnosed with cancer
A very bitter pill
But brave
A lioness
Kind and generous
A Princess
Nay, a Queen
Always now even though you've passed
My beautiful golden dream.
My lovely Gaynor

Golden Sunbeam
A crystal silver stream
Never let her disease defeat her spirit
So she is my inspirational woman
THE TRULY INSPIRATIONAL WOMAN OF MY LIFE.

8/3/22

What Makes A Man Great

It sounds trite
Because it's been said before
But what makes a man great
And if not great
Then makes him feel worthwhile
As if he's someone
He can achieve more, even slightly
Than he expected
A woman...
A woman that sees in him a spark
That he cannot see, his vision dark
A woman that tells him that he is loved
He is too good to give up on his gift
Even though his gift to him seems nought
A woman that cares when his body plays hell
Causing him stress and pain
For she is there again and again
Taking his hand
Stroking his brow and stemming his tears
A woman who stands at his side
That fills him with pride
And stays strong for him
When his strength fails.
That is what makes a man great

Not necessarily in power
Or money
Or in the gift she tells him he has
This is what makes a man great...
An even greater woman
A woman, a Lady like my own
My dear, sweet now sleeping love
My Gaynor.

The World Could End

The world could end
I wouldn't notice
Or even care
My world ended when you ceased being there
Here...
Here
With me
My world clouded
In bleakness shrouded the days
Cloaked the night even darker.
Once you brightened
Lightened even the stormiest skies
Brought smiles to my eyes
But now
Now I live in the past
My face a gloomy mask
The world could end
I wouldn't care
For I've lost my love and best friend.

Companionship

Companionship
The linking of minds
Of humour
Bonhomie
And when linked with love
Oh boy
It is something special
Like the person you are in companionship with
Special
Deep rooted
Irreplaceable.
But now our companionship
Is cemented in my mind and heart
Since you went to sleep
But my darling our love and companionship
Is breathing within me, deep.
It will always be special
The bond, your love and companionship
The best I could ever have had.
Always my sweet Gaynor
Always with me
Always will be
And I love, love, love you so much.

The Rocking Horse

The little girl sat on the end of her bed
Rocking gently backwards and forwards
Her long red hair swinging like a russet blanket
Her hands held clenched in front of her
"Careful over that log girl, careful"
She sat this way for quite a while
Eyes closed, imaging the beautiful carved rocking horse
That in her imagination she was very lightly rocking upon.

The little girl was with her brother, sister and parents
Her eyes focused on the windows of Christmas decorated shops
She stopped suddenly, eyes frozen upon the toy display
There, her imaginary rocking horse in all it's glory
Approaching the trove of treasures behind the glass
She gently said "Oh I would love that horse... it's beautiful".

A longing and dream never fulfilled in life, sad to say
But a conversation one day with me revealed her childhood wish
And I felt so sad for her
Then, as we know, this beautiful lady, once that girl
in a bedroom
Was my partner and love of my life.
I don't know if the first two segments happened
But I can imagine they did.

Sadly, we also know beautiful Gaynor passed away with cancer five years this February.

I passed a charity shop window two years after she went to sleep
And there, an auction for a rocking horse
A little worn but I imagine to Gaynor it would have been beautiful
So I put a big bid, determined to have it in the house we lived in.
It sits in the front room as some of you know
And I also know in my heart
Gaynor comes and sits upon it now
Gently rocking, her russet blanket of hair gently, gently swinging
Her eyes now looking upon that childhood desire
And of all things in my life now, it brings me joy
The joy of a wish for my beloved fulfilled.

10/1/25

Landscapes of Life

Landscapes of nature
Mosaics of life
Often are reflections of our existence
Steep, rugged mountain paths we have to climb
Landslides of rocks that are our tribulations...
Our struggles to overcome.
Cold, frozen rivers and woodlands...
The chills of sadness and sorrow that have come our way.
The harsh, blasting winds that throw us about...
The disappointments and letdowns we have struggled with.
The warm sunny days that have shone upon us...
The blissful warm friendships and love we have been blessed with.
The fragrance of flowers and tang of forests...
The scents of our loves and childhood hugs with parents.
Lakes, rivers and seas of varied colours and hues...
The deep liquid emotions we all experience.
And my favourite, most cherished landscape...
The years, though so sadly short, with my beloved Gaynor.
A picture of beauty herself, within and without.
Landscapes of our life impressed into our soul
Though if truth be told
Many do not realise.

16/2/25

Sing A Song

Sing a song of love
To one who is absent
Sing a song from the heart
For one whom we are apart.
Sing words of love and warmth
A song from deep inside
Sing a song of love and missing
For those who have died.
Sing a song of thanks
For the love they shared
Sing it clear and loud
Giving thanks that for you they cared.
Sing a song of love
A song so beautiful and true
And I'll sing my song in my heart
Grateful eternally that I found you.
Sing a song of thankfulness
That you shared their life
Sing a song so glorious
For sibling, parent, partner, husband or wife.
Sing that song every day
Sing it for those that have passed
Grateful for the life they had with you
Sing a song that will last.

31/12/24

Gaynor's Moon

I see the moon
In all its stages from this backroom
And occasionally from Gaynor's bedroom
Its silvered face
Sometimes a faint opalescent blue.
You loved looking at the moon
And seeing it since you passed
I always think of you looking and smiling
It was a friend to you
Even when asleep and curtains closed
It gazed down upon you
And I know you slept easy in that knowledge.
Through your time in hospital if you had a window bed
You would probably catch sight of your lunar friend
And in Myton too
It would have given you calming peace.
I feel sad when I look upon it
Missing my beloved Gaynor all the more
If that is possible
Knowing that where Gaynor wanders now
She will still see it
And I know she thinks of me whether she sees the moon or not
But she will know I am sending waves of love to her
Upon the moon's traverse in the heavens.

25/1/25

www.ingramcontent.com/pod-product-compliance
Lightning Source LLC
Chambersburg PA
CBHW052050070526
44584CB00017B/2113